W9-AZB-672

The KIDS' FUN-FILLED DICTIONARY

Written by Tracy Christopher
Created by Tony and Tony Tallarico

kidsbooks
Incorporated

Note to Parents and Teachers

The Kids' Fun-Filled Dictionary is the dictionary kids will want to read. Specially created to stimulate and educate young children, its humorous illustrations, story-like narrative, and wealth of fascinating facts will draw children into the world of learning—and keep them there! After all, children love to laugh, and *The Kids' Fun-Filled Dictionary* is full of joking good fun.

An excellent introduction to language, *The Kids' Fun-Filled Dictionary* is easy to read and focuses on topics familiar to children. At the same time, it is designed to help youngsters develop solid grammatical skills. It contains *more than 500 defined words*, including verbs, nouns, adjectives, and adverbs. Tenses for verbs are listed in bold type and then used in definitions, so that children become accustomed to the spelling and usage of various verb forms. Definitions also provide plural forms of nouns, as well as compound nouns, comparative adjectives, and superlatives.

With this kind of resource in their at-home library, beginning readers will learn the alphabet and will start to recognize the sounds that letters make—skills that will set children well on their way to reading and writing. As they develop on this path, children will build their vocabulary and learn early on how to use a dictionary. They will learn how to look for and find the things they want to know!

A book no child should be without, *The Kids' Fun-Filled Dictionary* will remain a long-lasting resource for the curious young mind—and a source of pleasure no child will want to put down.

Aa

Above

Melody is climbing a big hill. The sun and birds are **above** her. Her house is below her. It is at the bottom of the hill.

Accident

An **accident** is something that happens when you don't expect it. Tom fell while skating and hurt his knee. He had an **accident.**

Actor, Actress

Actors and **actresses** are men and women who play roles in movies, TV, and theatre. They like acting, or pretending to be other people.

Address

Your **address** shows people where you live. Your **address** should include your name, your street, city, state, and zip code.

Adult

You will be an **adult** when you are about 18 years old. Your parents are **adults**. They are grown-ups.

Air

We can't see or touch **air**. It is an invisible gas all around us. We breathe **air**, and birds fly through the **air**. Sometimes we blow **air** into balloons.

Airplane

With an engine and wings, **airplanes** can fly through the air. They carry people from one place to another. **Airplanes** land at the **airport.**

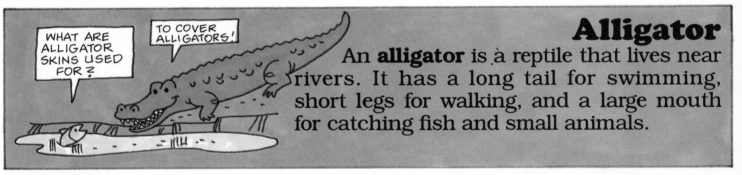

Alligator

An **alligator** is a reptile that lives near rivers. It has a long tail for swimming, short legs for walking, and a large mouth for catching fish and small animals.

Alone

When you are **alone**, you are by yourself. Tina's parents don't leave her **alone** in the house. When they go out, they call a babysitter.

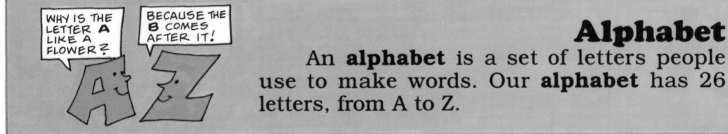

Alphabet

An **alphabet** is a set of letters people use to make words. Our **alphabet** has 26 letters, from A to Z.

Always

Jeremy loves bananas, so he **always** eats them. He eats them all the time.

5

Angry

When you feel **angry**, you feel mad. Sally got **angry** when her friends didn't want her to play on their team.

Animal

All things that are alive, except plants, are called **animals**. Flies, fish, birds, elephants, and alligators are **animals**. You are an **animal**, too!

Anybody

When Adam walked into the room and didn't see **anybody**, he called out: "Is **anybody** home? Is anyone here?"

Anything

Paul forgot his lunch, so he didn't have **anything** to eat. The teacher asked him if he wanted to eat something, and she gave him a sandwich.

Apartment

Heloise doesn't live in a house. She lives in an **apartment** building. Many people live in her building, and they all have different **apartments**. She lives with her family in **apartment** 15A.

Ask
(asks, asked, asking)

You **ask** questions when you want to know more about something. You can also **ask** people to do things for you. Brett **asked** her mom some questions about math. She **asked** her mom for help.

Bb

Baby

A **baby** is a very young child. Babies crawl before they learn to walk.

Back

Your coat has pockets on the front and a hood at the **back**. When you are at the front of the line, you are at the beginning. When you are at the **back**, you are at the end.

Bad

When something is **bad**, it is not right or not good. Hitting someone is **bad**. Food that you don't like tastes **bad** to you.

Bag

A **bag** is a soft, folding sack used to hold things. Bobbie's grandmother carries a **handbag**, or purse, to the store. Bobbie carries home her groceries in paper or plastic **bags**.

Bake
(bakes, baked, baking)

When you **bake** a cake, you cook it in the oven. You can **bake** lots of foods, like potatoes, chicken, and bread.

Ball

A **ball** is round and can be made of leather, rubber, wood, plastic, or metal. **Balls** are often used to play games—like tennis, baseball, basketball, and soccer.

Band

A **band** is a group of people, animals, or things. Some people form **bands** to play music. A rock **band** plays rock music and a brass **band** plays music for brass instruments, like trumpets and tubas.

Bandage

A **bandage** is a small patch made of plastic and cotton that protects a cut or scratch. Ace **bandages** are bigger and are used to give extra support to your muscles. Julie wears an ace **bandage** on her knee when she plays tennis.

Bank

You put money in the **bank** to keep it safe. Your piggy **bank** holds money while you save it.

Bath

When Jerry takes a **bath**, he uses soap and water to wash himself. He takes his **bath** in the **bathtub**, which is in the **bathroom**.

Beach

A **beach** is land close to an ocean or to other large bodies of water. A **beach** is usually covered with sand and rocks, and is a great place to play!

8

Bear

A **bear** is a large animal that lives on land, and that sleeps for part of the winter. **Bears** have thick fur, sharp claws and teeth, and eat animals and plants. Polar **bears** can run as fast as 35 miles per hour.

Because

You use the word **"because"** when you want to explain why. Jamie's game was cancelled **because** it was raining.

Bed

A **bed** is a place to sleep. Jack has his own **bedroom**. When it is **bedtime**, he gets ready for **bed**.

Bee

A **bee** is a black-and-yellow insect. **Bees** make honey, which you can eat. They also sting.

Before

Jane has to do her homework **before** she can watch TV. She must do her homework first, then she can watch TV.

Begin
(begins, began, begun, beginning)

When you **begin** something, you start doing it. Joey is **beginning** to learn how to read and to write.

Behind

Jenny is in front of the fence. The dog is **behind** the fence. He is on the other side. Jenny is not afraid, because the fence is between them.

Beside

The kittens played **beside** their mother. They played next to her, and she lay **beside** them.

Between

When you make a cheese sandwich, you put some cheese **between** two slices of bread. There is bread on both sides, and cheese in the middle.

Bicycle

A **bicycle** has two wheels, two pedals, and handlebars. Linda's dad doesn't drive to work. He rides his **bike** to work.

Big

African lions are **big** wild cats. They are **bigger** than mountain lions. But tigers are the **biggest** cats of all!

Bird

A **bird** is an animal with feathers. All **birds** lay eggs, and most birds can fly. Ostriches can't fly, but they can run—up to 40 miles per hour.

Birthday

Your **birthday** is the day of the year you were born. Leigh's **birthday** is December 11. She eats chocolate cake on her **birthday**.

Blind

Some **blind** people can't see at all, and others can barely see. Some **blind** people use guide dogs to help them go places.

LET'S GO TO THE PET FOOD STORE.

Boat

A **boat** floats in the water and carries people and things across the water. A ship is a very large **boat** that travels on the ocean. A canoe is a long, narrow **boat** that travels on rivers and lakes.

I'VE NEVER BEEN ON A BOAT.

Body

All animals have **bodies**. A mouse has a small **body,** and an elephant has a big **body**. The human **body** is shown in the picture on the next page.

I'M BIGGER THAN YOU!

REALLY!

Book

Books have pages, words, and pictures. This dictionary is a **book**. We buy **books** in **bookstores**, but we can also get **books** from the **bookshelves** in the public library.

THE BIGGEST BUILDING IN ANY TOWN IS THE LIBRARY BECAUSE IT HAS THE MOST STORIES.

Bottle

Bottles are made of glass or plastic and are used to hold liquids like milk, juice, and water. Babies drink from **bottles**.

LET'S DRINK UP.

11

THE HUMAN BODY

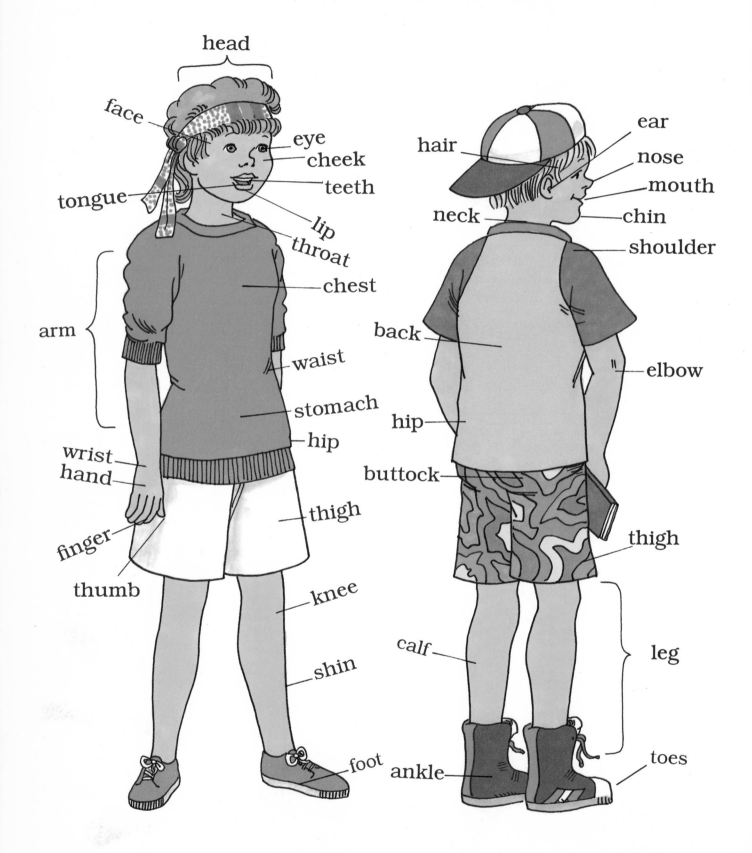

head

face

eye
cheek
teeth

tongue

lip
throat

chest

arm

waist

stomach

hip

wrist
hand

thigh

finger

thumb

knee

shin

foot

hair

ear
nose
mouth
chin
shoulder

neck

back

elbow

hip

buttock

thigh

calf

leg

ankle

toes

12

Break
(breaks, broke, broken, breaking)

When a window **breaks**, the glass falls out in pieces. When you **break** a radio, it no longer works.

Build
(builds, built, building)

Pete likes to **build** model airplanes. He's **building**, or making, one right now. When it is **built**, he will fly it in his yard.

Bulldozer

A **bulldozer** looks like a truck or tank with a big scoop or shovel in front. **Bulldozers** are used to move dirt, sand, and rocks, and to smooth out land.

Bus

People ride the **bus** to school or to work. **Buses** are large vehicles with many seats and room for lots of people. Matty is waiting for the **bus** at the **bus stop**.

Busy

When you are **busy**, you are doing something or you have a lot of things to do. Mike can't play this morning because he is very **busy** cleaning his room.

Butterfly

A **butterfly** is an insect with very colorful wings. The largest **butterfly**, Queen Alexandra's Birdwing, has a wingspan of 11 inches.

Cc

Calendar

FEBRUARY 25 IS A GREAT DAY!

Luke is looking at his birthday on the **calendar**. He can see the days of the week and the months of the year on the pages of his **calendar**.

Call
(calls, called, calling)

Denis is going to **call** his friends after school. He is going to **call** them on the phone and ask them to come over to his house.

I WANT THE GUYS TO COME OVER.

Camel

30 GALLONS! THAT'S A LOT OF LIQUID REFRESHMENT.

A **camel** is a desert animal. It has one or two humps on its back that contain fat—used for energy when food is short. **Camels** can drink up to 30 gallons of water at a time and go for months without drinking.

Camera

Josh is taking photos at the zoo with his **camera**. A **camera** uses light to make pictures on film. Josh can use a **video camera** to make videos.

SAY CHEESE... UH, I MEAN PEANUTS.

Camp

HELP!

Jean goes to summer **camp** in July. She sleeps in a cabin and plays outdoors. In August, Jean goes **camping** with her family. They set up a tent and build a **camp fire**.

14

Can (could)

When you **can** do something, you know how to do it, or you are able to do it. Dana **can** swim, but she **can't** go swimming today because she has a cold. She **couldn't** go swimming last week, either.

Can

Michael is throwing his gum in the **trash can**. **Cans** are made of metal or plastic, and they are used to store or to hold things.

Candy

Candy tastes sweet because it has lots of sugar. Bruce loves **candy,** especially chocolate, but he brushes his teeth after he eats it so that he won't get cavities.

Car

A **car** is a small vehicle that has an engine and four wheels. Jessica missed the bus, so her father had to drive her to school in the **car**.

Careful

Jorge is **careful** when he crosses the street. He waits for the light and he **carefully** looks around for cars. He watches what he is doing.

Carnival

A **carnival** has games, rides, and food stands. It is a place to have fun. Some schools have a **carnival**, or festival, in the fall or spring.

Carry
(carries, carried, carrying)

Molly **carries** books to school in her backpack. She also puts her lunch in a lunch box, so she can **carry** it to school, too. **Carrying** all these things makes Molly tired.

Castle

A **castle** is a large building that is both a house and a fortress. It has rooms for living, and it has thick walls for protection.

Cat

Tracy has two grown **cats** and one kitten at home. **Cats** are furry animals that purr. Lions, tigers, and leopards are wild **cats**.

Catch
(catches, caught, catching)

Jackie is playing **catch** with her friend. She **catches** the ball with her glove. Look! She just **caught** the ball!

Cave

Caves are made underground when water carves large holes in rock. **Caves** are dark, cold, and wet, but lots of fun to explore. Exploring a **cave** is called spelunking.

Cheetah

Cheetahs are wild African cats that have long, powerful legs. The fastest land animals on earth, they can run up to 70 miles per hour. **Cheetahs** have spots in their fur, which help them blend into the scenery.

Child

A **child** is a young boy or girl. **Children** become legal adults on their 18th birthday.

I CAN'T WAIT UNTIL I'M EIGHTEEN.

I'M GOING TO WEAR OUT THIS REMOTE CONTROL TRYING TO CHOOSE A PROGRAM.

Choose
(chooses, chose, chosen, choosing)

When you **choose** a TV program, you pick which one you want to watch. There are so many good programs, that Robert has a hard time **choosing** one.

Circus

People go to the **circus** to see clowns, acrobats, jugglers, and performing animals like dogs, elephants, and lions. Have you ever been to the **circus**?

WE WORK FOR PEANUTS.

EVERYTHING IS SO BIG IN THE CITY!

City

A **city** is a large town where people work, live, and go to school. New York, Chicago, and Los Angeles are large American **cities**.

Class

A **class** is a group of people who learn things together. Polly likes math **class.** Her father is also taking a **class** in math, after work. They do their homework together.

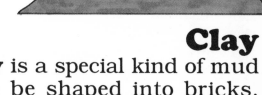

MY ANSWER IS 25.

MY ANSWER IS 26.

WELL ... IT WILL BE A BOWL ... SOON.

CLAY IS MUDDY.

Clay

Clay is a special kind of mud that can be shaped into bricks, tile, or pottery. Shelly is making a bowl out of **clay** in art class.

17

Clean
(cleans, cleaned, cleaning)

When something is **clean**, it is not dirty or messy. After Lawrence **cleaned** his room and **cleaned** out his closet, he had to take a bath to **clean** himself!

CLEANING YOUR ROOM IS A MESSY JOB!

Clock

WHAT'S FOR LUNCH?

A **clock** is a machine for telling time. Liz was hungry, and the **clock** showed that it was time for lunch.

Close
(closes, closed, closing)

Claire wants to **close** the door to her room. The door is open, and she wants to shut it.

WHEN YOU HAVE A LITTLE BROTHER WHO LIKES TO SNOOP AROUND, IT'S BEST TO CLOSE YOUR DOOR!

I MUST HURRY OR I'LL BE LATE!

SCHOOL

Close

Phil's house is **close** to school. His house is near school. If you look **closely**, you can see his school from his house.

Clothes

You wear **clothes** to protect your body. Some **clothes**, like ties, are used for decoration. You can see many types of **clothing** on the next page.

I DON'T HAVE A THING TO WEAR!

IF I HAD THE CHOICE BETWEEN HAVING A COLD OR GOING TO SCHOOL ... I'D RATHER GO TO SCHOOL ... ACHOOO!

ACHOOO!

Cold

Barbara forgot her sweater, so she was very **cold**. She was not warm. Poor Barbara. She caught a **cold**. **Head colds** are terrible!

CLOTHES

Color
(colors, colored, coloring)

Brian loves to **color** with crayons in his **coloring books**. He likes to use lots of **colors**. Red, yellow, and blue are **primary colors**. There are lots of other **colors**, like orange, purple, brown, black, and white. But Brian's favorite **color** is green.

Computer

A **computer** can be used like a typewriter to write. It can be used like a book to store information, and it can even draw. It can also be used to solve problems in math, science, or business. A calculator is a very simple **computer**.

Contest

A **contest** is like a game. James won the spelling **contest**, and he got a puzzle book as a prize. Maureen won the geography **contest**, and she got a globe as a prize.

Cook
(cooks, cooked, cooking)

When you make spaghetti, you **cook** the tomato sauce on the stove. You use heat to get it ready. Dan likes to **cook**, but he is a very messy **cook**.

Copy
(copies, copied, copying)

Ben is **copying** words. He is trying to make his words look like the ones in his book. He is learning how to write.

Corner

A piece of paper has four **corners**. A room has **corners** where the walls meet. Lila waited for the bus on the **corner** of Elm Street and Pine Street. She waited on the sidewalk, at the place where the two streets cross.

Costume

Children wear **costumes** for Halloween. They try to look like pirates or kittens or ghosts. Some of them are wearing masks as part of their **costume**.

Cough
(coughs, coughed, coughing)

When you **cough**, you push air out of your lungs to try to get rid of something that makes your lungs feel bad. Damian's grandfather caught a cold and **coughed** for days. He had a very bad **cough**.

Country

The **country** is land outside cities. There are more trees and not as many buildings in the **country**. Nations are also called **countries**, and they make up the world. The United States of America is a **country**, and Canada is a **country**.

Cow

Cows are farm animals. They eat grass and make milk that people drink. A **cow** can produce up to fourteen gallons of milk each day.

Crab

Crabs live in the ocean or the sea. To protect themselves, they have hard shells and pincers that hurt when they pinch. **Crabs** can't move forward—they can only move sideways!

Crane

Cranes are birds with very long necks, for catching fish underwater. There is also a machine named after this bird: A **crane** is used to lift materials high in the air when tall buildings are being constructed.

Crayon

Crayons are sticks of colored wax. Fred likes to draw and color with **crayons**.

Cross
(crosses, crossed, crossing)

Antonio can't **cross** the street by himself. He needs an adult to help him get from one side of the street to the other.

Crosswalk

A **crosswalk** is a set of white lines on the street, where it is safe for people to cross. When someone walks in the **crosswalk**, cars don't go past the painted lines.

Cry
(cries, cried, crying)

Harmony just fell down. She is **crying** because her knee hurts. She may **cry** all night.

Dd

Dance
(dances, danced, dancing)
Music has a rhythm, or beat. People **dance**, or move around, to the beat. Beth's grandparents are good **dancers**.

Danger
When something is **dangerous**, it can hurt you. Matches are **dangerous**. If there's a fire, you might be in great **danger**.

Day
There are seven **days** in a week: Monday, Tuesday, Wednesday, Thursday, Friday, Saturday, and Sunday. Maria goes to school five **days** each week.

Deaf
People who are **deaf** can't hear at all, or very little. Joey's father is almost **deaf**, but he can hear with his hearing aid.

Decide
(decides, decided, deciding)
Alek can't **decide** which tennis shoes to get. He can't make up his mind. Maybe his parents will **decide**, or choose, for him.

Deer

Deer are animals that live in the forest. They have long legs and rather long necks, so they can eat leaves and berries. A female **deer** is called a **doe**, a male is called a **buck**, and a baby is called a **fawn**.

Dentist

Christine is at the **dentist's** office. Her **dentist** is checking her teeth to make sure Christine doesn't have any cavities.

Dictionary

Dictionaries are special books that have lists of words and their meanings, or definitions. You are using a **dictionary** right now.

Different

These two dogs are very **different**. They are not alike. They don't look the same. One is bigger, and one is smaller. One has spots, and the other doesn't.

Difficult

Jeff is trying to tie his shoes, but it's not easy. Tying your shoes is a very **difficult,** or hard, thing to learn.

Dig
(digs, dug, digging)

The squirrel is **digging**. He is making a hole in the ground so he can bury his acorn. Later, if he can find it, he'll **dig** up the acorn.

24

Dinosaur

Dinosaurs lived millions of years ago, and there were many different kinds—both small and large. Some walked, while others flew.

Dirt

We need **dirt**, or soil, to make plants grow. When you play in the **dirt**, you get **dirty**. Aaron has been playing baseball, so his uniform is very **dirty**.

Do
(does, did, done, doing)

Sarah always **does** her homework. But yesterday, while she was **doing** it, she spilled milk on her workbook. She **didn't** spill it on purpose, though!

Doctor

Alex is at the **doctor's** office. The **doctor** is giving Alex a check-up. **Doctors** help you stay healthy, and they try to help you get well and feel better if you are sick.

Dog

Dogs and wolves are part of the same family, but **dogs** are tame and friendly. People keep **dogs** as pets. Eve's **dog** has just had puppies.

Dolphin

Dolphins live in water, but they aren't fish! Like people, they're mammals. They breathe air and give birth to their babies and nurse them on milk.

Dragon

Dragons are imaginary creatures. They are not real. **Dragons** are scary because they make fire come out of their mouths.

Draw
(draws, drew, drawn, drawing)

Sid is **drawing** a picture of a fire truck. Sid's baby brother is trying to **draw** too, but his **drawing** doesn't look like Sid's!

Dream
(dreams, dreamed, dreaming)

When you are asleep, you **dream**. **Dreams** play like movies in your head. When you're awake, you can **dream**, or think, about things. Last night, Sara Jane **dreamed** she was a famous singer. Today, she has been **dreaming** about the same thing at school!

Dress
(dresses, dressed, dressing)

Jerome is learning how to **dress** himself. He is learning how to put on his clothes. **Dressing** is hard when there are buttons!

Drive
(drives, drove, driven, driving)

Ted **drives** a bus. As the **driver**, he uses the bus to take people places. Ted's mom doesn't like to **drive**, so she rides the bus to work.

Drop
(drops, dropped, dropping)

Sue was so surprised to feel **raindrops** hit her nose that she **dropped** her juice. Her glass **dropped**, or fell, to the ground.

Ee

Eagle

An **eagle** is a large bird. It uses its good eyesight, big wings, and strong claws to fly down and grab mice and other small animals. The **bald eagle** has been an American symbol since 1782.

1782! WOW, I'M ALMOST AS OLD AS THE U.S.A.!

Earth

Earth is one of nine planets circling the sun. We live on the planet **Earth**. It is the only place we can live, so we have to try to keep it clean.

POLLUTION IS NO JOKING MATTER... KEEP OUR EARTH CLEAN!

Earthquake

When there's an **earthquake**, the ground shakes and breaks apart. **Earthquakes** can make buildings and bridges fall down.

THE ONLY SHAKES I WANT TO EXPERIENCE ARE THE ONES YOU DRINK!

Eat
(eats, ate, eaten, eating)

Betty is learning to **eat** with a spoon. When she **eats**, she puts food in her mouth, chews it, and swallows it.

NOT ALL OF BETTY'S FOOD GOES INTO HER MOUTH!

Elephant

Elephants are very large animals from Africa and Asia. They use their trunks to reach the grass, leaves, and fruit they eat. They also use their trunks like hoses, to drink and to spray water.

Elevator

Elevators are machines that carry people and things up and down the inside of buildings. Carl lives on the 15th floor, so he takes the **elevator** up and down every day.

Enjoy
(enjoys, enjoyed, enjoying)

The children really **enjoyed** themselves at Ed's birthday party. They really had a great time. Ed always **enjoys** having parties.

Escape
(escapes, escaped, escaping)

To **escape** means to get away from or out of something. Jana's gerbil **escaped** from its cage when Jana was cleaning the cage.

Exercise

Your body needs **exercise** to stay healthy. When you walk, run, swim, or ride your bike, you are getting lots of **exercise**.

Exit

Exit signs show you the way out of a place. Hildy's mom wanted to leave the store, so she looked for an **exit** sign.

Explain
(explains, explained, explaining)

When you **explain** something, you try to help people understand more about it. When David was learning how to play checkers, his grandfather **explained** the rules of the game.

Ff

Family

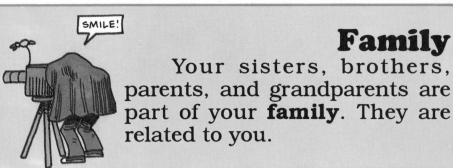

Your sisters, brothers, parents, and grandparents are part of your **family**. They are related to you.

Farm

A **farmer** raises animals for food and grows fruit, vegetables, and grains like wheat or barley. The land he uses is called a **farm**.

Favorite

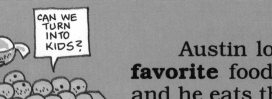

Austin loves oranges. They are his **favorite** food. He prefers to eat them, and he eats them all the time.

Feel
(feels, felt, feeling)

Have you ever **felt**, or touched, snakeskin? It **feels** dry and soft, but you might **feel** too scared to touch a snake.

Feelings

You have lots of different **feelings** or emotions. Sometimes you **feel** sad or angry or hurt or happy or excited. Making new friends gives you a great **feeling**.

FAMILY

FARM

Fight
(fights, fought, fighting)

If you really don't agree with something your friends say or do, you might **fight** or argue with them. When Tiffany **fought** with her brother, her mother made them apologize.

Find
(finds, found, finding)

Anthony looked under a log for his pet frog, who was lost. He didn't **find**, or locate, him. He **found**, or discovered, a lot of bugs.

Fire

When something is burning in the neighborhood, the **fire alarm** rings in the **fire station**. **Fire fighters** run to their **fire truck** and rush to fight the flames of the **fire**.

Fireworks

On July 4, you can watch **fireworks**. They explode with a loud noise into bright lights in the sky. But **fireworks** can be very dangerous, so you must be careful.

Flower

Flowers are the brightly colored parts of plants. **Flowers** help make and hold the plant's seeds. In the spring, there are lots of **flowers**.

Fly
(flies, flew, flown, flying)

Birds **fly**, or move through the air, by flapping their wings. Airplanes **fly** through the air, but use their wings mostly for balance.

Food

All living things need **food** to live, grow, and stay healthy. Soil is **food** for plants, grass is **food** for cows, and worms are **food** for robins. Can you name some of the **foods** people eat?

Forest

A **forest** is a large area of land with many different trees, plants, and animals that need one another to live and grow.

Forget
(forgets, forgot, forgotten, forgetting)

Ron didn't remember to bring his baseball glove today. He **forgot** his glove, so he had to borrow one from Frank. Ron is so **forgetful**, he always **forgets** his glove.

Fossil

Plants and animals trapped inside rocks were alive millions of years ago. They are now **fossils**. Footprints and other traces of life that have turned into stone are also **fossils**.

Fox

A **fox** is a small wild animal that lives in mostly wooded or bushy areas. **Foxes** eat plants and small animals.

Freeze
(freezes, froze, frozen, freezing)

When water **freezes**, it turns into snow or ice. While **freezing**, it changes from a liquid to a solid.

FRUIT

Friend

A **friend** is someone you like and who is nice and **friendly** toward you. Alan has lots of **friends** who like to play games or just hang out and talk with him.

Frog

When a tadpole develops legs and lungs for breathing air, it becomes a **frog**. Adult **frogs** live near water to keep their skin wet and cool.

Fruit

Trees and other plants make **fruit** to hold, or contain, their seeds. **Fruit** is often sweet and good-tasting, so animals and people carry it off and eat it. The seeds get scattered, and more trees grow.

Full

Patty's water bottle was **full** when she began the bike race. But she drank all her water, so now her bottle is empty.

Fun

Richard had a lot of **fun** at the circus. He really had a good time. He laughed so much at the clowns—they were really **funny**!

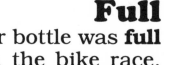

Furniture

Chad and his friends made a clubhouse in the basement. They needed **furniture**, so Chad's mom gave them some chairs and a cardboard box to use as a table.

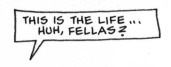

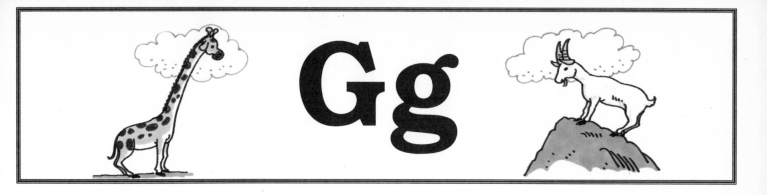

Gg

Game

When you play in teams, or play according to a set of rules, you are playing a **game**. Chess is a **board game**. Hopscotch and soccer are **games**, too.

I THOUGHT WE WERE GOING TO PLAY SOCCER?

BUT I BROUGHT MY CHESS SET WITH ME.

Garbage

Anything that you don't want or use gets put in the **garbage**. There are probably things in your **garbage can** that you can recycle—paper, plastic, glass, and metal.

DON'T PUT THINGS THAT CAN BE RECYCLED IN ME!

Garden

MY GARDEN LOOKS GREAT THIS YEAR. MY TOMATOES ARE ALMOST AS BIG AS MY BLISTERS.

Ilana grows flowers, vegetables, and fruit in her **garden**. She has planted tulips, tomatoes, and strawberries in land that she has decided to use as her **garden**.

Gasoline

Gasoline is a liquid made from oil that we use as fuel for cars and other engines. We call **gasoline** "gas," but real **gases** are vapors like air and the helium in balloons.

I'M FULL OF GAS!

Gentle

WHAT DO YOU CALL A KITTEN AFTER IT'S THREE DAYS OLD?

FOUR DAYS OLD!

Wayne's cat had kittens. He has to be very **gentle**, or careful, when he holds them. He has to hold them **gently** so they won't get hurt or scared.

35

Giraffe

A **giraffe** is the tallest animal in the world. **Giraffes** can grow 18 feet tall and have very long necks, so they can reach high branches and eat the leaves they like so much.

WE ALSO HAVE A GREAT VIEW FROM UP HERE.

PRETTY GIRLS DON'T BOTHER ME...I WISH THEY WOULD!

Girl

Girls are female children. When **girls** become adults, they are called women.

Give
(gives, gave, given, giving)

Mary is **giving** Nicole half of her candy bar. She is offering half of it to Nicole. She has already **given** Nicole a piece of gum.

THIS IS FOR YOU.

THANKS.

IS THAT FOR ME?

Go
(goes, went, gone, going)

John **goes** to school by bus. He takes the bus to get from his house to school. John is **going** to give his teacher an apple today. He plans to give her an apple.

Goat

Goats are small farm animals with short horns and long hair under their chins. Female **nanny goats** produce milk for their babies, called **kids**.

DO YOU NEED A SHAVE?

THIS IS A VERY PRECIOUS PIECE OF JEWELRY!

HOW MANY COINS DID IT TAKE TO GET IT OUT OF THE MACHINE?

Gold

Gold is a precious, or rare, metal because it is found in small quantities. **Gold** can be hammered and molded. It has been used to make jewelry for thousands of years.

Good

Martin loves ice cream. Vanilla is **good**, strawberry is even **better**, but chocolate ice cream is the **best**.

Gorilla

Gorillas are the greatest of all apes—the adult male can weigh up to 400 pounds. They live in Africa, but are in danger of disappearing from the Earth, because of hunting and loss of living space.

Grasshopper

Grasshoppers are insects that can hop long distances using their powerful hind legs. They can also make a loud humming or buzzing sound by rubbing their back legs together.

Groceries

A **grocery store** is a place where people buy **groceries**, or food. To save paper, remember to take old **grocery bags** with you when you go shopping, so you can carry your new **groceries** home.

Grow
(grows, grew, grown, growing)

Plants need soil, water, and sunlight to **grow**—to get bigger and to develop. Animals need food and water to **grow**.

Gymnasium

People exercise and play sports in **gymnasiums**—buildings or rooms that have sports equipment. In school, kids go to the **gym** to play.

Hh

HE HAS A HABIT OF NOT PAYING ATTENTION.

WHAT WAS THAT?

Habit

Brushing your teeth is a good **habit**—a good routine, a good thing to do over and over again. Smoking is a very bad **habit**, because it can be bad for your health and is hard to stop.

Half

Carol broke her brownie in **half**, so that there were two pieces that were the same size and shape. She ate one of the **halves**, and gave the other **half** to her friend.

BROWNIES CAN BRING GOOD FRIENDS EVEN CLOSER.

OAK   MAPLE

Happen
(happens, happened, happening)

The accident **happened** at five o'clock. It took place on the corner of Oak and Maple Streets. Accidents **happen** all the time there, because there's no traffic light.

Happy

It's Elliot's birthday today, so he is very **happy**. He feels good, and he is looking forward to his birthday dinner.

ACTUALLY I'M LOOKING FORWARD TO MY BIRTHDAY CAKE.

OUCH!

Hard

Rocks are **hard**. They don't break into pieces or change shape easily. It is very **hard,** or difficult, to break a rock with your hands. Using a hammer might be easier.

Hate
(hates, hated, hating)

When you **hate** someone, you feel so angry and hurt that it's hard to be around that person. When you **hate** something, you don't like it at all. Greg **hates** spinach, but he doesn't **hate** his little sister.

Hear
(hears, heard, hearing)

You **hear** sounds with your ears. If you sit still and listen, you may **hear** birds singing and cars going by in the street.

Heart

Your **heart** is a big muscle inside your chest that pumps blood through your body. If you put your hand in the middle of your chest, you can feel your **heart** beating.

Hide
(hides, hid, hidden, hiding)

The children run off to **hide**, to play a game of **hide-and-seek**. Luisa is **hiding** in the closet. She is out of sight, and she is hoping no one will find her.

High

Hawks and eagles fly **high** in the sky, so **high** you can barely see them. Owls are heavier, so they fly much lower to the ground.

Hippopotamus

A **hippopotamus** is a large, plant-eating animal with a huge mouth. **Hippo** babies weigh 100 pounds when they are born.

Hole

Nicholas worked so hard digging a **hole**, or opening, in the ground, that he made a **hole** in his glove!

Holiday

People don't have to go to work or to school on **legal holidays**. **Holidays** like July 4th and Labor Day are times to relax and have fun with family and friends.

Honest

George is **honest**. He doesn't tell lies, and he is sincere. He tries to say exactly what he thinks and feels about things.

Hop

(hops, hopped, hopping)

Kangaroos **hop**, or jump, from place to place. People can **hop** on one leg, or **hop** moving both legs together at the same time.

Hospital

Hospitals are buildings with special equipment to take care of people when they are sick or need special help. Most people are born in the **hospital**.

Hot

Streets feel **hot** in June when the sun warms them up. They feel **hotter** in July, and **hottest** in August, when the sun shines on them all day.

Hotel

Hotels are large buildings that have rooms with beds. People stay in **hotels**. When you travel, you can camp out or you can stay in a **hotel**.

House

Houses are buildings where people live. You sometimes call your **house** your **home**. A house is shown on the next page.

Hug
(hugs, hugged, hugging)

Lian **hugged** her mother when she got home from school. She put her arms around her mother and gave her a big **hug**, or squeeze.

Hungry

When you are **hungry**, you really want to eat something. When you feel **hungry**, your body is telling you that it needs food. Babies often cry when they are **hungry**.

Hurry
(hurries, hurried, hurrying)

When you **hurry**, you try to move or to do something quickly. When it began to rain, Rachel **hurried** home because she didn't want to get wet.

Husband

Kyle's mom is getting remarried. The man she is marrying, her new **husband**, will be Kyle's stepfather.

HOUSE

Ii

Ice

When the temperature falls below 32°F, water freezes and becomes **ice**. **Ice cubes** and **icicles** are hard and cold, but they melt when you touch them and when the temperature rises.

SNOWMEN WILL MELT WHEN THE TEMPERATURE RISES.

Idea

It's Anne's birthday, and her mother has a great **idea**, or plan. She will invite Anne's friends over for cake and ice cream. That's a wonderful **idea**.

Insect

Insects are animals with six legs and hard bodies. There are more species, or kinds, of **insects** than of any other animal. Ants, bees, and flies are **insects**.

YOU CAN CATCH MORE FLIES WITH HONEY THAN YOU CAN WITH VINEGAR!

SO? WHO WANTS MORE FLIES?

Invent
(invents, invented, inventing)

In 1867, Alexander Graham Bell **invented**, or created, the first telephone. He made something useful that no one else had ever made.

NOW I CAN PHONE IN MY ORDER TO SAM'S PIZZA.

HI, MOM! I INVITED A FEW DOZEN FRIENDS TO COME OVER!

A FEW DOZEN!

Invite
(invites, invited, inviting)

Eric **invited** his friends to his house after school. He asked them if they wanted to come over.

43

Jj

DON'T WORRY, DEAR. NEXT MONTH IS YOUR BIRTHDAY.

THAT'S RIGHT! I FORGOT.

Jealous

People sometimes feel **jealous** when they see something they want but can't have. They might also feel **jealous** if they feel left out. Brianna was **jealous** of her baby brother on his birthday.

Jewel

Jewels are rare or precious stones that people use to decorate themselves or objects. A queen is especially proud of the diamonds, rubies, and other **jewels** in her crown.

SOMETIMES I WISH I COULD JUST WEAR JEANS AND A T-SHIRT.

I'D LIKE EVERYONE TO WELCOME OUR NEWEST STUDENT.

HI!

Join
(joins, joined, joining)

The teacher told us a new boy was going to **join**, or be part of, our class. The boy **joined** the class the next day.

WE HID THE CHALK UNDER THE ERASERS.

Joke

Our class told **jokes**, or funny stories, on April Fool's Day. We also played a **joke** on the teacher—we hid all of her chalk.

AN UMBRELLA COMES IN HANDY IN THE JUNGLE.

Jungle

Jungles have trees, plants, and animals, like forests do, but it is hotter and more humid in the **jungle**. In fact, it rains a little every day in the **jungle**.

Kk

I FEEL SAFE AND WARM.

Kangaroo

Kangaroos from Australia have powerful legs for jumping and a long, thick tail for balance and support. A female **kangaroo** carries her baby in a pouch, where it is safe and warm.

Keep
(keeps, kept, keeping)

Burt's uncle gave him a dollar in a birthday card and said Burt should **keep**, or store, the dollar in a piggy bank. Burt **kept** the birthday card—he didn't lose it or throw it away—but he spent the dollar.

I USED THE DOLLAR TO BUY A PIGGY BANK.

ARE YOU IN THERE, THUMBELINA?

Key

Keys are used to open locks or doors or boxes. Thumbelina was so small that she could fit through the **keyhole** and hide in the locket on Lucy's **key chain**.

Kick
(kicks, kicked, kicking)

Carlos **kicked** the soccer ball. He hit it so hard with his foot that his toes hurt, but he made a goal!

OUCH!

I LIKE CARROTS! DO YOU?

Kind

There are many **kinds** of vegetables. Which ones do you like? Which types? Broccoli? Carrots? Asparagus?

KITCHEN

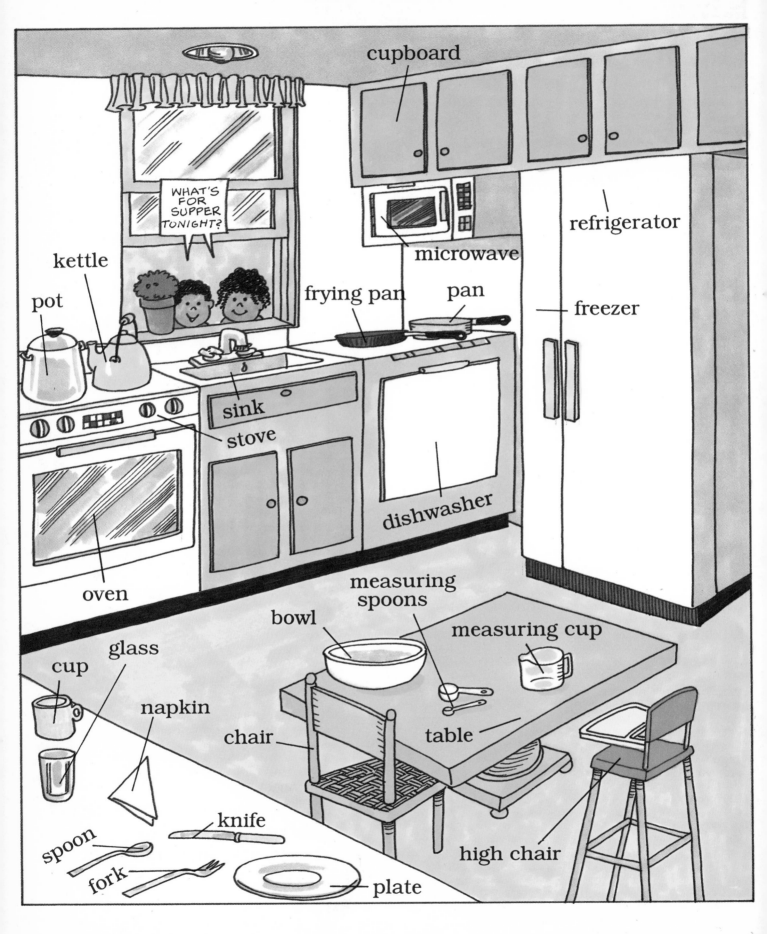

Kind

Ethan is always very **kind** or nice to older people. He is **kind** enough to hold open doors and to ask people if they need help.

Kitchen

Kitchens are rooms where food is cooked. Houses, hospitals, hotels, and restaurants all have **kitchens.** A picture of a **kitchen** is on the opposite page.

Kite

Kites can be made from plastic, paper, fabric, and wood. They must be light and have enough flat surfaces to catch the wind, so they can fly.

Knight

The first **knights** were warriors who fought under an elected leader. In the Middle Ages, **knights** fought for powerful lords or kings. They were rewarded with land, money, and titles.

Knock
(knocks, knocked, knocking)

When the wolf **knocked** at the little pigs' door, no one would let him in, so he tried to **knock** down the house by blowing it over.

Know
(knows, knew, known, knowing)

Do you **know** your telephone number? Are you sure? Could you give your number without looking or asking someone else? Then you **know** it!

47

Ll

ONE DAY WE SHOULD TRY TO DISCOVER WHY KIDS DON'T WALK AROUND PUDDLES.

Laboratory

People who work in **laboratories** learn about science and make new discoveries. **Laboratories** have the equipment to run tests and to do experiments.

Ladder

Firefighters use **ladders** to rescue people. Painters climb **ladders** to paint ceilings. You might have a **step ladder** in the kitchen to reach the top shelves of cabinets.

I LIKE THE COLOR.

Large

Whales are very **large** animals. They are **larger** than any other animal. Blue whales are the **largest** animals to have ever lived. They can be up to 110 feet long.

THAT'S ONE THAT I HOPE GETS AWAY.

Last

The letter "Z" is the **last**, or final, letter of our alphabet. "A" is the first letter of the alphabet. "Z" is at the end, and "A" is at the beginning.

I'M THE LAST LETTER OF THE ALPHABET.

Laugh
(laughs, laughed, laughing)

Whenever Ian's puppy jumps up and licks his face, Ian **laughs**. He **laughs** because the puppy is tickling him and because he's happy.

YOU MAKE ME LAUGH.

Laughter

At the circus, whenever the clowns chase each other, you can hear the happy sound of the children's **laughter**.

Lead
(leads, led, leading)

Leaders are often chosen by groups to help them decide what to do and how to achieve their goals. Martin Luther King, Jr., **led** the Civil Rights Movement. The president **leads** the United States.

I'M LEADING THE PARADE.

THEY WENT THAT WAY.

Learn
(learns, learned, learning)

People go to school to **learn**, to find out things they didn't know before. Maybe you are **learning** how to read and write at school.

WE'RE LEARNING ABOUT WORDS JUST BY READING THIS DICTIONARY.

Leave
(leaves, left, leaving)

Kate was having so much fun at the game, she didn't want to **leave**. She didn't want to go anywhere else. She wanted to stay at the game.

BUT, KATE! THE GAME IS OVER! THE HOT DOG VENDOR IS ALL SOLD OUT! THEY'RE TURNING THE LIGHTS OUT.

SO?

Left

It took Lucas a long time to learn that his **left** hand is the one he draws with and eats with. He is **left-handed**.

ALL MY FRIENDS CALL ME LEFTY.

Library

Scott goes to the **library** when he wants to pick out more books to read. The **librarians**, people who work at the **library**, help him choose his books.

ONE THING LIBRARIANS CAN'T DO IS WHISTLE WHILE THEY WORK.

QUIET PLEASE

Lick
(licks, licked, licking)

Cats **lick** themselves with their tongue to keep clean. People eat ice-cream cones by **licking** the ice cream as it melts.

I'LL LICK UP WHAT FALLS.

Light

When it's time for bed, you turn off the **light**, or lamp, so you can sleep. If it's too dark, you can turn on the **night-light**.

WHY IS IT THAT THE ONE WHO SNORES ALWAYS FALLS ASLEEP FIRST?

Z-Z-Z-Z-Z-Z-Z-

Light

Flowers and feathers are **light**; they don't weigh very much. Big sticks and rocks are much heavier. They are much harder to pick up and carry.

DO YOU WANT TO TRADE?

Lightning

Lightning is a flash of light made during a storm, between clouds or a cloud and the ground.

EXCUSE ME!

PARDON ME!

Like
(likes, liked, liking)

Jordan **likes** to play soccer. He really enjoys himself when he plays. He thinks it's a lot of fun. He'd **like** to play every day.

I GET A KICK OUT OF SOCCER!

ME TOO!

Listen
(listens, listened, listening)

Trevor **listens** to stories his teacher tells during storytime. He is quiet, so he can **listen** carefully and imagine what is happening in the story.

HI, GUYS.

THE WOLF DECIDED TO PAY THE THREE LITTLE PIGS A VISIT.

Live
(lives, lived, living)

Neal's fish **live** in an aquarium. They eat, grow, and develop in the water of their fish tank. They have never **lived** anywhere else.

Lizard

Lizards are reptiles that have a long tail and four short legs. **Lizards** have to run fast to catch the insects they eat. The largest **lizard** is the Komodo dragon of Indonesia, which is 10 feet long and weighs 300 pounds.

Long

Abbe has **long** hair. Joy's hair is **longer** than Abbe's. Laurie has the **longest** hair of all.

Look
(looks, looked, looking)

Matt always **looks** both ways before he crosses the street. While **looking**, he makes sure he doesn't see any cars. Then he knows it's safe to cross the street.

Lose
(loses, lost, losing)

Maggie has **lost** two of her front teeth. She doesn't have them anymore, but she has the dollar that the tooth fairy left under her pillow.

Love
(loves, loved, loving)

Nat **loves** his little brother. He really likes his little brother, and feels happy when he is with him.

Mm

Magic

I'LL NEVER TELL HOW THIS MAGIC TRICK IS DONE!

Eugene saw a **magician** performing **magic tricks** on television. The **magician** was doing things that seemed impossible, like making rabbits disappear. It was **magic**.

Mail

Your **mail carrier** puts **mail**—letters, postcards, bills, and magazines—in your **mailbox**. You probably get **mail** every day except Sunday.

I'M FULL.

Make
(makes, made, making)

HAPPY, MOTHER'S DAY!

MOM

Lynn **made** a card at school for her mom for Mother's Day. She **made**, or created, the card using paper and markers. Lynn loves to **make** things in art class.

Man

When a boy is 18 years old, he becomes a legal adult, and he is called a **man**. **Men** are grown-up boys.

I'M A GROWN-UP BOY!

Many

HI, JIM!

Jim has **many** friends. He has a lot of friends. **Most** of his friends are on his soccer team, but he has some **more** friends in his class at school.

Map

Maps are drawings that show where things are located. **Street maps** show all the streets of a city. **Bus maps** show all of the routes and stops of the bus system. **World maps** show where all of the countries in the world are.

Mask

Children wear **masks** on their faces for Halloween, to change the way they look—to disguise themselves. Doctors and dentists wear **face masks** to avoid spreading germs.

Match
(matches, matched, matching)

These socks don't **match**. They are not the same. They are different from each other.

Maybe

Judy's family might go camping during the summer vacation. **Maybe** they will go. Perhaps they will go—but they are not sure.

Meal

People usually eat three **meals** each day—**breakfast** in the morning, **lunch** in the afternoon, and **dinner** in the evening.

Mean

Daniel was **mean** to his little brother. He wasn't very nice or kind. He wouldn't let him play with his toys or his friends. He hurt his brother's feelings.

53

Medicine

When you are sick, your doctor writes an order for **medicine**—pills or liquids—to make you feel better or to help you get well. Your parents give you the right amount of **medicine** by following the doctor's instructions.

TAKE TWO OF THESE AND CALL ME IN THE MORNING.

I'M A PARTIAL-METAL-AND-PARTIAL-JUNK CAR.

Metal

Steel, aluminum, iron, gold, and silver are **metals**—minerals from the earth that have been made into tough but bendable materials that last a long time. Parts of cars and other vehicles are made from **metal**.

Middle

When you begin a game of hockey, you put the hockey puck in the **middle**, or center, of the ice. A player from each of the two teams tries to hit the puck away from the **middle** toward his or her team.

I DON'T MISS ALL THE TIME!

Miss
(misses, missed, missing)

Manuel tried two times to hit the ball with the bat, but he **missed** both times. He didn't hit the ball on the first two swings, but he did on the third swing.

Mistake

Gary made two **mistakes**, or errors, on his spelling test. He spelled two words incorrectly, but he spelled everything else right.

I SPELLED MY NAME RIGHT.

IT'S A GOOD EXCHANGE.

Money

People use **money**—paper bills and metal coins—to buy things.

Monkey

Monkeys are primates, like apes, but they are much smaller and many have tails. Most live in trees, and they eat leaves, fruit, insects, or small animals. A baboon is a large **monkey**.

EVERY NOW AND THEN, A PIZZA WOULD BE A PLEASANT CHANGE.

REMEMBER, MONSTERS ARE MAKE-BELIEVE.

Monster

Monsters are frightening creatures that appear in myths, fairy tales, and in science-fiction and horror films.

Month

The calendar year is divided into 12 periods called **months**: January, February, March, April, May, June, July, August, September, October, November, December.

I LIKE DECEMBER

I'M GETTING DIZZY FROM ORBITING.

Moon

The **moon** travels around, or orbits, the Earth. It takes about 30 days for the **moon** to orbit the Earth. Most of this time, you can see only part of the **moon**. But sometimes you can see the full **moon**.

Museum

Museums take care of and display important collections of valuable objects. **Art museums** collect paintings, drawings, and sculpture.

I WONDER IF A MUSEUM WOULD DISPLAY MY DRAWING?

UH! THAT SOUNDS AWFUL! ARE YOU PLAYING WITH YOUR KNUCKLES?

VERY FUNNY!

Music

Musicians are people who are very good at playing **music**. There are many types of **music**—classical, folk, jazz, blues, gospel, rock, rap. Sounds that have rhythm, harmony, or melody are considered **musical**.

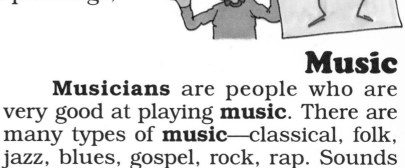

SO MANY PUPPIES...
SO MANY CHOICES OF NAMES.

I'M
SPOT!

Name
(names, named, naming)
Glenn wants to **name** his new puppies, but he doesn't know what to call them. The one with the spots on his back will be **named** Spot, of course.

Nature
All animals, plants, bodies of water, and land masses are part of **nature**. Anything that is not man-made is **natural**.

I'M
NATURAL.

SO AM
I.

I WISH ALL
MY RELATIVES
LIVED NEARBY.

Near
Susanna's grandmother lives **near**, or close to, Susanna's house. But her uncle lives far away in another city.

Neat
Henry keeps his room **neat**, or tidy. He picks up his clothes and his toys. But his sister Melissa's room is very messy!

MELISSA,
DO YOU
WORK AT
BEING
MESSY OR
DOES IT
COME
NATURAL
TO YOU?

KEEP YOUR
NEIGHBORHOOD
CLEAN.

Neighborhood
The streets, stores, schools, and other buildings around your house are part of your **neighborhood**. Your **neighborhood** is the area of the city or town you live in.

News

New events, or happenings, are called **news**. The daily **newspaper** has articles, stories, and pictures that describe what is happening. The paper gives you the **news**.

IT ALSO GIVES YOU THE COMICS.

HE'S TAKING FOREVER!

I'LL HAVE CHOCOLATE CHIP... NO, I'LL HAVE MOCHA NUT... NO, I'LL HAVE STRAWBERRY...

Next

Steve is **next** in line to get ice cream—there is only one person in front of him.

Night

When the sun goes down, the **night** comes. You sleep at **night**. **Nighttime** is very dark, but sometimes there is light from the moon and stars.

I'M OUT FOR MOST OF THE NIGHT.

ME TOO.

WAH!

Noise

A **noise** is a loud sound. When balloons pop, they make a lot of **noise**. When people talk or laugh loudly, they are very **noisy**.

North

North is one of the four directions given on a map or a compass. The United States is a country on the continent of **North America**. Canada is to the **north** of the U.S., and Mexico lies to the south.

WE ALL KNOW IN WHAT DIRECTION THE NORTH POLE IS.

I ONLY COUNTED 29!

YOU FORGOT TO COUNT YOURSELF.

Number

Numbers are used for counting. If Adriana counts all the children in her class, she will count 30 students. Thirty is the **number** of students in her class.

Oo

Ocean

About three-fourths of the Earth's surface is covered by salt water. This large body of water is called the **ocean**. It is made up of the Pacific, the Atlantic, the Indian, the Arctic, and the Antarctic **oceans**.

Octopus

An **octopus** is a sea animal that has a soft round body and eight long arms, or tentacles, for catching sea creatures.

I'D BE GREAT IN A BASEBALL FIELD!

MY RADIO IS BROKEN!

NO IT'S NOT! IT'S JUST TURNED OFF!

Off

When the radio is **off**, you can't hear voices or music coming from it. It is not playing. But, if you turn it on, you can listen to a lot of different stations.

Old

Mr. Williams is an **old** man now, and his baseball glove is very **old**. But when he was young, and when his glove was new, he was a great ballplayer.

YOU CAN LEARN A LOT FROM AN OLD PERSON!

DO NOT DISTURB SERIOUS GOOFING OFF IN PROGRESS!

Open

When the door to Debbie's room is **open**, you can see her bed, her desk, and her toys on the floor. But when her door is shut, or closed, you can't see her things.

Opposite

Gordon is going up the stairs, and Grady is going down. They are going in **opposite** directions.

Otter

Otters are animals that live in and near water. **Otters** have shiny, furry skin, a long sleek body, and webbed feet—perfect for swimming.

Out

Jason put money in the soda machine, but the coins came back **out** of the coin return. A light came on saying that the machine was **out of order**—it wasn't working.

Outdoor

Corinne has an **outdoor** swimming pool. In the summer, Corinne and her friends like to play **outdoors**— outside—in the pool. But, when it rains, they all come indoors—inside.

Outside

The **outside,** or outer part, of a watermelon is smooth and green. The inside, or inner part, is juicy and red—and very good to eat.

Over

If you stand on the floor of your room, the ceiling is **over** your head, and the floor is under you. The ceiling is **overhead** and the floor is underneath.

Pp

I THINK I HAVE TOO MUCH STUFF IN THIS BACKPACK.

Pack
(packs, packed, packing)
Before he leaves for school, Graham **packs** his books, his homework, and his lunch in his **backpack**.

Paint
(paints, painted, painting)
Charyl uses brushes and **paints** to **paint** on paper, wood, or canvas. When **painting** with her fingers, she uses **finger paints**.

MY MOM STARTS TO LOOK WORRIED WHEN I'M FINGER PAINTING!

CHARYL! DON'T TOUCH ANYTHING!

GOODNIGHT.

Pajamas
Lindsay wears **pajamas** at night. **Pajamas** are special, comfortable clothes that people wear to bed.

Paper
Paper is made from plant fibers, or pulp, the sturdy material in plants and trees that makes them stand up. The pages of this dictionary are made of **paper**.

I LIKE TO DRAW ON PAPER.

PARROTS ARE TROPICAL BIRDS WITH BRIGHTLY COLORED FEATHERS AND...

Parrot
Parrots are tropical birds with brightly colored feathers and long tail feathers. Some **parrots** are good at imitating sounds and can be taught to repeat certain words.

Party

Stephen is having a birthday **party**. He has invited his friends and family to celebrate. They will eat special foods and have fun together at his celebration.

Patient

IF I WEREN'T SO PATIENT I'D HAVE SHORTER HAIR.

Vanessa has long hair. She has to be **patient**—calm and still—while her mother combs it out. She has to sit **patiently** and wait until her mother is finished.

Pay
(pays, paid, paying)

Woody's dad **paid** cash for Woody's new skates. He gave the salesman money in exchange for the skates. Usually he **pays** with a check or credit card.

THANKS FOR PAYING FOR THE SKATES, DAD.

Peace

WORLD PEACE DOESN'T HAVE TO BE JUST A DREAM.

If the world were at **peace**, no one would be fighting, and there would be no wars.

Penguin

Penguins are black-and-white birds that eat fish and that live in or near water. **Penguins** can't fly, but they have webbed feet and flippers, like seals, for swimming quickly.

HOW DO THEY TELL EACH OTHER APART?

People

LET'S ALL SMILE FOR THE READER.

There are four **people** in Sophie's family. The **person** holding the banana is Sophie.

Photograph

Cameras make **photographs** by exposing film to light, so that an image from outside is reproduced on film. People who take **photos** are called **photographers**.

Pick
(picks, picked, picking)

For awhile, Lauren couldn't decide whether to wear her jeans or her green dress to school. Finally, she **picked**, or chose, the green dress.

Picnic

The Tinsley family has packed a lunch in a **picnic basket**, and they are going to have a **picnic**. They are going to eat outdoors.

Picture

A **picture** is a painting, drawing, or photograph. The refrigerator is covered with Althea's latest **pictures**.

Piece

When Rusty's Aunt Mary makes fried chicken, Rusty always eats more than one **piece**, or part, of the chicken. Sometimes he eats 3 or 4 **pieces** but never the whole chicken.

Pigeon

Pigeons are birds with fat bodies and short feathers. **Rock pigeons** live in most cities. **Carrier pigeons** can be used to carry small messages tied to their feet.

Planets

The Earth is one of nine **planets** that move around the sun. **Planets** are made of metals, rocks, and gases. They are shaped like huge spheres, or balls. The nine **planets** are Mercury, Venus, Earth, Mars, Jupiter, Saturn, Uranus, Neptune, and Pluto.

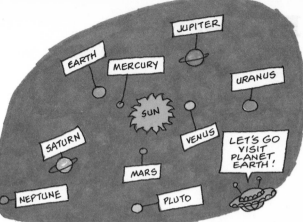

Plant
(plants, planted, planting)

Ruth's parents are **planting** a garden. They are putting tomato plants in the ground.

Plant

Right now, the tomato **plants** have roots in the earth, and stems, leaves, and flowers growing above ground. Later, the **plants** will have fruit—tomatoes!

Plastic

Plastics are made from liquid chemicals that are poured or shaped to make bags, bottles, and lots of other things. **Plastics** are useful because they are tough and don't break easily.

Play
(plays, played, playing)

The children like to **play** on the **playground**. Felix is **playing** on the jungle gym with Johnny.

Player

There are nine **players** on a baseball team. A **player** is a person who plays a game or who participates in a sport.

Police

Police officers work for the city police department. Their job is to arrest or stop people who are breaking the law. The police are also there to help and protect you.

Polite

Joel is polite and kind. He always says "please" and "thank you." He tries to help people and to treat them politely, to think about their feelings.

Pollute
(pollutes, polluted, polluting)

If you throw garbage into a pond, you pollute the water. You make it so dirty that fish and plants can't live in it. Pollution in our world is a big problem.

Pond

The pond in the park has water lilies and goldfish in it. Ponds are small bodies of water, much smaller than lakes.

Prefer
(prefers, preferred, preferring)

For breakfast, Amber prefers to eat pancakes. She likes cereal, too, but pancakes are her favorite.

Pretend
(pretends, pretended, pretending)

Vanette is pretending to be a famous singer. She knows that she is not a pop star, but she is making believe that she is.

Pretty

Reggie's dad brought home a lot of **pretty** flowers. His mom chose the **prettiest**, or most beautiful, flower to wear in her hair.

Prize

When you win a game or a contest, sometimes you get a **prize**. Alicia won **first prize** at the science fair. She got a ribbon and a microscope as **prizes**.

Promise
(promises, promised, promising)

Curtis **promised** to be home before dark. He said that he would be home, and he will make sure to keep his **promise**.

Protect
(protects, protected, protecting)

Raincoats and umbrellas **protect** you from the rain. Football and bicycle helmets **protect** your head from getting hurt.

Proud

When Carly helped her little sister learn how to read, her parents were very **proud** of her. They felt good about what Carly had done. She felt **proud**, too.

Puddle

Puddles are small pools of water. When it rains a lot, **puddles** form on the sidewalk and in the street.

65

Pull
(pulls, pulled, pulling)
Warren is **pulling** a red wagon. He is walking ahead and moving the wagon toward him.

IT WOULD BE EASIER TO PULL IF YOU WERE WALKING, ABNER.

I NEVER WANT TO BE PUNISHED AGAIN. I'LL NEVER LIE!

Punish
(punishes, punished, punishing)
Caroline lied to her parents. They **punished** her by not letting her play with her friends for a week. They **punished** her, hoping that she would not lie again.

Puppet
Puppets are dolls moved by strings or by your fingers. **Puppets** can look like people or animals. People who perform with **puppets** are called **puppeteers**.

HELLO, DUMMY!

WHO SAID THAT?

I'M GOING TO PUSH THIS CART ALL THE WAY TO THE COOKIE AISLE.

Push
(pushes, pushed, pushing)
Andrew **pushes** the cart at the grocery store. He moves the cart ahead of him, away from his body.

Put
(puts, put, putting)
Charles doesn't know where he **put**, or set down, his glasses. But they are on top of his head, right where he **put** them.

WHO TOOK MY GLASSES? I CAN'T FIND THEM! SO SOMEONE MUST HAVE TAKEN THEM!

I NEED A SIX-LETTER WORD THAT STARTS WITH A "P" AND MEANS "GAMES OR PROBLEMS THAT ARE DIFFICULT."

Puzzle
Puzzles are games or problems that are difficult, but fun, to work on. Susanna likes **jigsaw puzzles**, but Marcus prefers **crossword puzzles**.

Quarter

A **quarter** is one-fourth of something. With U.S. money, a **quarter** is one-fourth of a dollar bill. You need four **quarters** to make one dollar.

Queen

A **queen** is the wife or widow of a king. Princes and princesses are sons and daughters of **queens** and kings. There aren't many real **queens** left in the world.

Quick

Greyhounds are very **quick**, or fast, dogs. They run **quickly**—over 40 miles per hour.

Quiet

Jesse was playing **quietly**. He had to be **quiet** because his brother was sleeping. He was making very little noise.

Quilt

A **quilt** is a blanket or bed covering made of many layers and pieces of fabric, or material. **Quilts** are soft and usually very warm.

Rr

Race
(races, raced, racing)
Two runners are **racing** for the finish line. They are running as fast as they can, because they want to win the **race**.

Radio
Radios are machines that receive **radio signals**. **Radios** change these signals into the voices or music you hear when you tune into a **radio station**.

Rain
Rain is water that falls from the clouds in the form of **raindrops**. If the sun shines while it is **raining**, an arc of colored light, called a **rainbow**, appears in the sky.

Reach
(reaches, reached, reaching)
Gail has to stand on a chair to **reach** the cereal. She has to stretch out her arm to **reach** the cereal box.

Read
(reads, read, reading)
Malcolm is learning to **read**. He is learning how to say and how to understand words that are written in books and on signs.

Ready

Kathy is getting **ready** to leave for school. She has everything she will need for school today. She is prepared. But she isn't quite **ready** to leave, yet. She has to eat her breakfast first.

YOU CAN'T START YOUR DAY WITHOUT A GOOD HEALTHY BREAKFAST.

Remember
(remembers, remembered, remembering)

WHERE IS THE LOST AND FOUND DEPARTMENT?

UH...? I DON'T REMEMBER!

To **remember** is to recall something felt or learned. When Jake got lost at the store, he **remembered** to ask a security officer for help. Later, he **remembered** feeling scared.

Repair
(repairs, repaired, repairing)

Jennifer's bike had a flat tire. Her older sister helped her **repair**, or fix, it. Jennifer's sister is good at **repairing**, or fixing, things.

...AND WHEN YOU'RE DONE, MY TEDDY BEAR IS LOSING ITS STUFFING!

Reptile

EEK!

Snakes, lizards, and alligators are **reptiles**—cold-blooded animals with a backbone, and scales or plates for skin.

Rescue
(rescues, rescued, rescuing)

The firefighters **rescued** some people and animals trapped in the burning building. They saved them from harm.

FIRE-FIGHTERS ARE BRAVE PEOPLE.

Restaurant

I'D LIKE A TABLE NEAR A WAITER!

Rhonda's family eats out in a **restaurant** on very special occasions. **Restaurants** are places where you can buy and eat a meal.

Rhinoceros

A **rhinoceros** is a large, grass-eating animal from Africa or Asia. It has very thick skin and one or two horns on its nose.

IF WE HAD A RHINOCEROS, I WOULDN'T HAVE TO MOW THE GRASS.

I LEARNED TO RIDE MY BIKE WHEN I WAS ONLY SIX YEARS OLD.

Ride
(rides, rode, ridden, riding)

Tammy **rides** her bike to the park, but she **rides** the bus to school. To **ride** is to travel on or in something from place to place.

Right

In America, people drive on the **right** side of the road. In England, people drive on the left side of the road.

MAYBE THAT'S WHY YOUR BROTHER IS SUCH A BAD DRIVER.

YES. HE THINKS HE IS STILL IN ENGLAND.

513!

YOU'RE RIGHT!

$57 \times 9 = ?$

Right

Thea answered the math problem correctly. She got the **right** answer—the true, or correct, answer. She didn't get the wrong answer.

Ring
(rings, rang, rung, ringing)

The phone is **ringing**. It is making a humming noise, like bells do when they **ring**.

MY EARS ARE RINGING!

NO, SILLY! IT'S JUST THE TELEPHONE!

I'M STANDING ON THE RIVERBANK.

KEEP STANDING ON THAT RIVERBANK!

River

A **river** is a very large stream of running water that is deep and wide. The land or channel underneath the **river** is called the **riverbed**. The land at the sides, or edges, of a **river** is called a **riverbank**.

Road

Roads are hard, smooth surfaces for cars and other vehicles to travel on. **Roads** and highways connect big cities and the land between them.

IF IT WEREN'T FOR ROADS, I'D HAVE NOTHING TO TRAVEL ON!

ALL I NEED IS A COUPLE OF THOUSAND MORE ROCKS... AND I CAN BUILD A HOUSE.

Rock

Rocks are large pieces of compact earth, metals, and minerals. **Stones** can be used to make fences, houses, and roads. **Pebbles** and **stones** are small **rocks**.

Rough

Tree bark feels **rough**, or bumpy, uneven, and prickly. Glass in a window feels smooth. Carpet feels **rough**, and a bathtub feels smooth.

FIDO, HOW DOES THIS BARK FEEL?

RUFF-RUFF!

CAN YOU FIND IT IN YOUR HEART TO FORGIVE ME?

Rude

Keith got angry at his friend. He said unkind things. He was very **rude**, or impolite. He will have to apologize for acting so **rudely**.

Rule

The **rules** of a game tell the players what they can and cannot do. Schools, families, and other communities also have and make **rules**.

NO! THE RULES SAY THAT THE BATTER CAN'T USE A TENNIS RACKET.

THAT'S A SILLY RULE.

BEING A CAT, I DO A LOT OF RUNNING.

Run
(runs, ran, run, running)

To **run** is to move forward quickly, using your legs. When the dog began to **run** toward the cat, the cat **ran** up a tree.

Ss

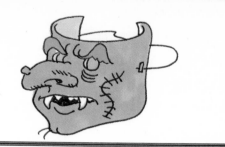

IT'S ONLY A LITTLE RAIN!

Sad

To feel **sad** is to feel upset or unhappy about something. Diane felt **sad** and disappointed when the school picnic was rained out.

Safe

When you feel **safe**, you feel protected. It might be **safe** to go outside by yourself, but it's **safer** to be with friends. It is **safest** to have an adult with you.

I FEEL SAFE WHEN I'M WITH MY PARENT.

I FEEL SAFE WHEN I'M WITH MY FRIEND.

I SHOULD REALLY EAT THEM BOTH—TO MAKE SURE THAT THEY BOTH TASTE THE SAME.

Same

These two cookies are the **same**. They are exactly alike. They are identical. You can't tell any differences between them.

Save
(saves, saved, saving)

Rhoda is **saving** her money. She's not spending it. She's putting it in a safe place. After she has **saved** enough money, she will buy a bicycle.

KEEP AN EYE ON MY MONEY, MR. PIG.

I LOVE HALLOWEEN.

FEET, RUN!!

Scare
(scares, scared, scaring)

On Halloween, the witch at the haunted house **scared,** or frightened, the youngest children. She wasn't really a witch, but her costume was **scary**!

72

School

A **school** is a place for learning new things. You learn how to read and write in **school**. Later, you might go to **law school** or **cooking school**.

YOU'RE NEVER TOO OLD TO LEARN!

Science

WELCOME TO MY CLASS... I AM PROFESSOR FRANKENSTEIN!

GULP!

Scientists study how natural objects and forces work and how they work together. Biology, chemistry, physics, and astronomy are some of the **natural sciences**.

Scissors

You use **scissors** to cut paper and other things. **Scissors** have two cutting blades and handles shaped in loops for your fingers.

SINCE SCISSORS ARE SHARP AND POINTY, YOU MUST BE CAREFUL WHEN USING THEM.

Sea

I'M SALLY AND I'M LOOKING FOR SEASHELLS AT THE SEASHORE.

Seas are very large bodies of salt water. Sometimes, oceans are called **seas**, too. The land at the edge of the **sea** is called the **seashore**.

Season

The year is divided into **seasons**—winter, spring, summer, and fall. But the weather is not the same wherever you go. In winter, it is often warm in Florida, while it's cold in New York.

HMMM... MAYBE I SHOULD LIVE IN FLORIDA DURING THE WINTER, NEW YORK DURING THE FALL, TEXAS DURING SPRING AND MAINE DURING SUMMER?

Selfish

I WAS SELFISH AND NOW I'VE GOT A STOMACH ACHE!

When you are being **selfish**, you aren't thinking about anyone but yourself. Stacy ate a whole bag of candy by herself. She seemed **selfish** for not sharing.

Send
(sends, sent, sending)

When you **send** a letter or a package, you have it carried from one place to another. Monica's uncle **sent** her a birthday present through the mail.

ONE BIRTHDAY GIFT FOR MS. MONICA!

Shadow

MY SHADOW IS BIGGER THAN ME!

Your body blocks the sunlight trying to reach the ground and makes a **shadow**, or dark shape, on the ground. Trees and other objects make **shadows**, or **shade**, too.

Shape

Triangles, circles, squares, and rectangles are geometric **shapes**. The **shape** of a thing is the outline or form it makes in space.

A STOP SIGN'S SHAPE IS CALLED AN OCTAGON.

I'VE GOT EIGHT SIDES.

STOP

Share
(shares, shared, sharing)

IT'S FUN TO SHARE.

To **share** is to let someone use or take part of something that belongs to you. Celia forgot her book, so Alex **shared** his book with her.

Sharp

Knives and scissors have **sharp** blades and points. They can cut or pierce things easily. When knives and scissors are dull, they may need **sharpening**.

MY LITTLE BROTHER IS DULL. CAN HE BE SHARPENED?

VERY FUNNY!

Short

IT'S NOT EASY BEING SHORT.

WHERE ARE YOU HUGH?

When something is **short**, it is not long or tall. Hugh is the **shortest** boy in the class. He has **short** hair. His hair is **shorter** than anybody else's.

Show
(shows, showed, shown, showing)

The art teacher **showed** our drawings to our parents. She let our parents look at them. She is also going to **show**, or display, them on the walls of the art room.

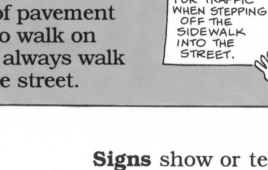

Shy

You might feel **shy** or a little scared when meeting new people. Angela felt very **shy** on the first day of school, but she made new friends in math class.

Sidewalk

The **sidewalk** is a strip of pavement or concrete made for people to walk on beside the street. You should always walk on the **sidewalk**—never in the street.

Sign

Signs show or tell people what to do. A **stop sign** tells people to stop. Look at all the **signs** on the next page.

Silly

To be **silly** is to do funny or foolish things. The kitten became so excited that it began to do **silly** things like chase its tail.

Sing
(sings, sang, sung, singing)

When you **sing**, you make music with your voice. Janice **sang** a song for her friend Wendy.

SIGNS

Sit
(sits, sat, sitting)

To **sit** is to rest the bottom part of your body on a chair or on the floor. The children **sat** in a circle around the storyteller.

Size

Knowing the **size** of something is a way of measuring how big or little it is. Theo grew so much over the summer that he needed a new pair of jeans in a bigger **size**.

Skate
(skates, skated, skating)

To **skate** is to glide quickly along a surface using a pair of **skates** on your feet. **Ice skates** have metal blades for **skating** on ice. **In-line skates** have wheels for **skating** on the pavement.

Skunk

Skunks are furry animals that look a little like black cats with a white stripe down the back. **Skunks** make a very bad smell when they are excited or scared.

Sky

The **sky** is the space above the land that looks blue and has clouds. **Skyscrapers** are very tall buildings that got their name because they seem to touch or scrape the **sky**.

Slow

Tortoises walk very **slowly**. They don't move quickly or fast. Many other animals are **slow**, such as sloths and snails.

Smart

Toby's puppy is **smart**. He is always alert and learns how to do things quickly. But he's not as **smart** as Toby. Toby can read, write, and solve problems.

IF I WERE IN THE THIRD GRADE, MAYBE I COULD READ AND WRITE, TOO!

MY NOSE KNOWS!

Smell
(smells, smelled, smelling)

You **smell** or recognize odors with your nose. Isaac knew he was having hot dogs for dinner because he could **smell** them cooking.

Smile
(smiles, smiled, smiling)

When you **smile**, your mouth and face show that you are happy or amused. Marilyn **smiled** when the class sang "Happy Birthday" to her.

IT'S A GOOD THING I BRUSHED MY TEETH.

SNOWFLAKES ADD UP TO SNOWMEN!

Snow

When rain hits very cold air, it freezes into tiny flakes called **snow**, and these **snowflakes** fall to the ground. After a heavy **snowfall**, the ground looks white.

Someone

People use the word **someone** or **somebody** to talk about a person they don't know or can't name. Mrs. Harrison said, "**Someone** took the last brownie, but I don't know who it was."

THAT SOMEONE WASN'T ME!

SOMETHING TELLS ME THAT I'M IN TROUBLE...OVER A BROWNIE!

Something

People use the word **something** when they don't want to name or can't name the exact thing they are talking about. Mr. Harrison said, "I wanted **something** to eat, and that brownie looked good."

Sometimes

When you do something **sometimes**, you do it every now and then, but not all the time. Maureen's family **sometimes** goes camping in the summer. **Sometimes** they go visit Maureen's grandmother instead.

SOMETIMES I GO CAMPING WITH MY GRANDMOTHER.

Somewhere

I'D LIKE TO GO SOMEWHERE WHERE LITTLE PESTY BROTHERS AREN'T AROUND.

People use the word **somewhere** when they don't want to name or can't name the place they are thinking about. We would like to go **somewhere** this weekend, maybe to the movies or to the park.

Sorry

When you feel **sorry**, you feel sad and upset about something. Ronny was **sorry** that he broke a window playing catch. He said he was **sorry** to the neighbors.

I GUESS I DIDN'T PLAY CATCH TOO WELL!

South

THAT BIRD IS FLYING SOUTH.

South is one of the four directions given on a map or on a compass. Mexico and Brazil are countries to the **south** of the United States.

Space

Space is the enormous area that exists beyond the earth's atmosphere. **Spacecraft** are vehicles that travel in **space**.

MISSION CONTROL... THERE'S CERTAINLY A LOT OF SPACE IN OUTER SPACE!

CAN YOU SAY DOG?

GIVE ME A BREAK... I'M FIVE YEARS OLD NOW!

Speak
(speaks, spoke, spoken, speaking)

To **speak** is to use your voice to make words. Children usually learn to **speak**, or talk, before they are three years old.

Special

When something is **special**, it is unique, different from anything else, or more valuable. Diego loves to read, and his comic books are very **special** to him.

Squirrel

Squirrels are small, furry animals with bushy tails. **Squirrels** are related to other rodents, like mice or rabbits, and they live where there are trees.

Stand
(stands, stood, standing)

To **stand** is to stay on your feet without moving. The bus was so crowded that Travis had to **stand**.

Star

Stars are visible in the night sky. They look like tiny lights. **Stars** are balls of gases, metals, and rocks, like the planets in our solar system.

Start
(starts, started, starting)

To **start** is to begin something. Sherry **started** a drawing of some flowers, but she didn't like it. She didn't finish it, and **started** drawing a cat instead.

Stay
(stays, stayed, staying)

To **stay** is to remain somewhere for awhile. Blythe told her dog to **stay** outside while she went into the shop. The dog **stayed** there and waited a very long time.

Stop
(stops, stopped, stopping)

When you **stop** doing something, you don't do it anymore. Ginny's mom **stopped** cleaning Ginny's room. She doesn't do it anymore, because Ginny cleans her room herself.

Story

Stories are told to teach people about things that happened long ago or about things that are happening now. Most **stories** in the newspaper are true and real. Most fairy tales are imaginary, or invented.

Stranger

Strangers are people you don't know. You shouldn't talk to or go anywhere with **strangers**.

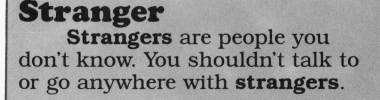

Street

Streets are hard, paved surfaces for cars and other vehicles traveling around the city.

String

String is strong, thick thread. Dylan uses a big roll of thick **string** to fly his kite.

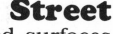

Strong

Elephants are **strong** animals. They can pull and carry heavy things. **Strong** elephants can lift 600-pound logs with their trunks.

Submarine

Submarines are warships that can travel both above and completely below water. **Submarines** can travel 1300 feet below the surface of the water.

IF YOU HAD A SUBMARINE, WHERE WOULD YOU KEEP IT?

UH... IN MY BATHTUB?

IT CERTAINLY FEELS HOT FOR SOMETHING THAT IS 93 MILLION MILES AWAY!

Sun

Our **sun** is a huge star that provides the Earth with heat and light. The **sun** is thousands of times bigger than the Earth, and it is about 93 million miles away.

Surprise

A **surprise** is something you don't know about ahead of time. It **surprises** or amazes you when it happens. At her **surprise party**, Virginia was so **surprised** that she laughed and cried at the same time.

HER REACTION IS A SURPRISE TO ME.

THANK YOU VERY MUCH!

TASTEBUDS ARE COOL!

Sweet

You have special tastebuds at the front of your tongue that tell you when something tastes **sweet**. Chocolate cake tastes **sweet**. Lemons don't. They taste sour.

Swim
(swims, swam, swum, swimming)

When you **swim**, you move through the water without touching the bottom. Elvira learned to **swim** in **swimming class** at the **swimming pool**.

COME ON IN... THE WATER IS FINE.

Swing
(swings, swang, swung, swinging)

To **swing** is to move back and forth or to move around in a circle. The children were **swinging** crazily, twisting the **swings** in the park.

SWINGING IS FUN!

Tt

Take
(takes, took, taken, taking)
Colleen's mom said she could **take,** or have, two cookies. Colleen **took,** or chose, the biggest ones.

Talk
(talks, talked, talking)
Roberto's baby brother can't **talk** yet. He can't use words to say anything. But Roberto **talks** to him anyway.

Teach
(teaches, taught, teaching)
Ms. Jones is our music **teacher**. She is **teaching** us how to sing as a group. She will also **teach** us to play musical instruments.

Team
A **team** is a group of people who compete in a game or a sport together. There are nine players on a baseball **team**, and two **teams** compete in a game.

Tease
(teases, teased, teasing)
Eli **teased** his dog. Eli held out a bone to the dog, but never gave it to him.

Teenager

Teenagers are people between the ages of 13 and 19. Janelle's brother is a **teenager** and goes to high school.

Telephone

Your **telephone**, or **phone**, has electrical wires that carry the sound of your voice to another place. Colin **phoned**, or called, his uncle Phil in Chicago.

Television

Your **television**, or **TV**, has electrical wires and tubes that convert electricity into light and sound. There were only about 10,000 **television sets** in the United States in 1945. Now, almost everyone has a **TV set**.

Test

A **test** is used to measure or find out about something. When teachers give you **spelling tests**, they want to find out if you can write certain words correctly.

Thermometer

A **thermometer** measures how hot or cold something is. It measures temperature. Your body's normal temperature is 98.6 degrees Fahrenheit.

Thick

Valerie has **thick** hair. She has a lot of hair. It makes a **thick**, or wide, braid down her back. Mr. Fields doesn't have **thick** hair. In fact, his hair is so thin, you can see right through it to his head.

Think
(thinks, thought, thinking)

What is Jody **thinking** about? She is **thinking**, or imagining, that she is a famous actress. She is not **thinking** about her math homework.

I AM VERY HAPPY TO RECEIVE THIS AWARD FOR MY LATEST FILM. I'D LIKE TO THANK MY MATH TEACHER.

Thirsty

When you are **thirsty**, you want something to drink. Your body needs lots of water, so you should drink a lot when you are **thirsty**.

IF I DRINK ANY MORE WATER, I'LL JUST FLOAT AWAY!

Through

The runners knew that they were almost **through**, or finished, with the race when they went **through**, or across, the last tunnel.

I THINK I'M THROUGH NOW!!

Throw
(throws, threw, thrown, throwing)

When you **throw** a softball, you push it forward out of your hand. You try to **throw**, or direct, it to a certain person, and you hope the ball will go that far.

THROW ME THE BALL!

Thunder

When the electricity from lightning pushes through the air, there is **thunder. Thunder** sounds like a loud boom or a cracking or rumbling noise.

GEE, WITH ALL THIS THUNDER... DO YOU THINK IT'LL RAIN?

BOOM! BOOM!

IT ALL DEPENDS ON THE WEATHER!

Ticket

A **ticket** is a piece of paper saying that you have paid to do something. You need **tickets** to travel in planes and trains. You also need **tickets** for the movies.

THESE AREN'T MOVIE TICKETS, SIR... THEY'RE AIRLINE TICKETS!

UH-OH! I HAVE A FEELING THAT YOUR BROTHER IS TRYING TO BOARD AN AIRPLANE WITH THEATER TICKETS!

Tight

Zoe grew so much over the summer that her old school clothes were too **tight**, or too small. Zoe got new clothes, but they were too loose, or too big, for her.

Time

We have invented a system called **time** to measure our experiences and to remember things. Clocks and calendars measure **time**. Minutes, hours, days, weeks, months, and years are all units for measuring **time**.

Tired

Lance was so **tired** after his game that he took a nap. When you are **tired**, you want to sleep or to rest your body. When you get **tired** of doing something, you don't want to do it anymore.

Toad

Toads look like frogs, but they have dry and bumpy skin. **Toads** develop as tadpoles in water, and they lay their eggs in water. As grown **toads**, they spend most of their time on land.

Today

Craig didn't go out yesterday, on Friday, because he was at school. He can't go out **today**, on Saturday, because he has to clean his room. Maybe he will go out tomorrow, on Sunday.

Tool

You use **tools,** like hammers and saws, to make or to fix things. You can keep **tools** in a **tool shed** and work on a **tool bench**. For now, Pete keeps his **tools** in a **tool box**.

Touch
(touches, touched, touching)

When you **touch** something, you feel it with your hands or with another part of your body. When Sheila **touched** the duckling, it felt warm and soft.

Tourist

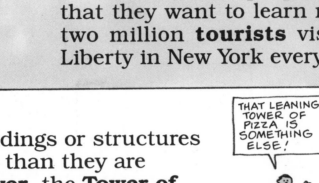

Tourists are people who visit a place that they want to learn more about. Over two million **tourists** visit the Statue of Liberty in New York every year.

Tower

Towers are buildings or structures that are much taller than they are wide. The **Eiffel Tower**, the **Tower of London**, and the leaning **Tower of Pisa** are famous **towers**.

Town

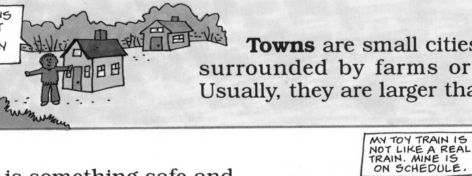

Towns are small cities. **Towns** are surrounded by farms or open land. Usually, they are larger than villages.

Toy

A **toy** is something safe and fun for a child to play with. Rosie's trains are her favorite **toys**.

Trade
(trades, traded, trading)

When you **trade** something, you exchange it, or give it, for something else. At lunch, Grace **traded** her sandwich to Casey for a bowl of spaghetti.

Train

Trains have an engine that pulls a series of boxcars along tracks, or rails. Today, **trains** carry more freight, or things, than they carry people.

Treasure

Things that are very rare or valuable are called **treasures**. Sometimes these rich and precious things are hidden or buried. **Treasure maps** tell you where to look for **buried treasure**.

Tree

Trees are some of the largest plants. **Tree roots** help **trees** stand upright and absorb water. **Tree trunks** support **tree branches** and leaves.

Trick

When you play a **trick**, or joke, on someone, you make them believe something that isn't true. Zach **tricked** his mom into believing the flowers were from him, when really his dad was the one who brought them home.

Trip

Danika's class is taking a **trip** to the museum. They are going to see photos taken by people on **trips**, or voyages, around the world.

Trouble

Ruben is having **trouble** reading. He is having problems reading. Ruben is **troubled,** or worried, about it, but he is getting help from his teacher.

Truck

Trucks are large vehicles with lots of space for carrying things. **Dump trucks** carry materials at construction sites, dumping them in the right places.

I NEED A TRUCK TO MOVE ALL MY TOYS!

True

True stories tell what really happened. They are accurate, sincere, and honest. It is better to tell the **truth** than to tell lies.

THAT'S THE TRUTH... ULP!!!

Trust
(trusts, trusted, trusting)

Your parents **trust** you not to get into dangerous situations. **Trusting** you, they believe that you will behave well.

WE'RE TRUSTING YOU TO BE GOOD WHILE WE'RE AWAY.

BEHAVE YOURSELF WITH THE BABYSITTER!

BABY-SITTER?

IF I HAD A TUGBOAT, IT WOULD BE THE MOST POWERFUL OF ALL TUGBOATS.

Tugboat

Tugboats are sturdy boats with powerful motors. **Tugboats** can push or pull much larger boats through the water.

Turn
(turns, turned, turning)

The wheels of your bicycle **turn**, or rotate, around. The handlebars help you **turn**, or change direction. When sharing your bike, you give other people a **turn**, or chance, to ride, too.

WHO'S TURN IS IT?

MINE.

NO! IT'S MY TURN!

NO! MINE!

COME ON OUT, MR. TURTLE. NO REASON TO BE AFRAID OF ME.

Turtle

Turtles are reptiles that have a hard, protective shell. Most **turtles** can hide their legs, tails, and head in their shell when they are scared. Tortoises are **turtles** that live on land.

Uu

Unhappy

Clifton is **unhappy** because his dog got lost. He is sad, disappointed, and angry. He is not happy.

Unicorn

A **unicorn** is a mythical or imaginary animal. Drawings of **unicorns** show them as white horses with a long horn growing out of their forehead. **Unicorns** were once thought to be magical animals.

YOU'RE REAL AND I'M NOT!

Up

GOING UP!

Toni lives on the fourth floor of her building. She could walk **upstairs**, but she has decided to take the elevator **up** to her home on the fourth floor.

Use
(uses, used, using)

You **use** crayons or pencils when drawing a picture. You can also **use** markers or paints.

I DON'T MIND YOU USING CRAYONS. JUST DRAW ON PAPER... NOT THE WALLS!

Usual

HE'S USUALLY TIRED WHEN HE GETS HOME FROM WORK!

Andy's dad **usually** works five days a week. He normally, or generally, works from Monday through Friday. His **usual,** or normal, work week gives him Saturday and Sunday off.

Vv

ALL THIS TIME I'VE BEEN EATING FLOWERS, ROOTS, AND SEEDS! WHO KNEW?

Vegetable

Plants have parts that people eat, called **vegetables**. Broccoli is the flower of a cabbage plant. Carrots are roots. Beans are actually seeds. Tomatoes are the fruit of tomato plants. See the next page for lots more!

Veterinarian

Veterinarians are doctors who take care of animals. They help protect animals from diseases, and try to heal them when they are sick.

I THINK MY DOG HAS A COLD.

WE COME FROM A TINY VILLAGE.

OUR VILLAGE'S LIBRARY HAD TO CLOSE. SOMEONE TOOK OUT THE BOOK!

Village

Villages are much smaller than towns and cities. Surrounding **villages** are farms and open land. **Villagers** are people who live in **villages**.

Visit
(visits, visited, visiting)

When you **visit** a place, you go there to see something or someone. When Carmen's cousin came to **visit**, Carmen's family made a special **visit** to the zoo.

HI, GUYS!

WOW! IT'S BIGGER THAN THE TWO OF US PUT TOGETHER.

Volcano

IT'S A GREAT PLACE TO ROAST HOT DOGS!

Way below the Earth's surface, there is hot liquid rock. When the pressure there builds up, the melted rock is pushed up through an opening, called a **volcano**. The **volcano** erupts.

91

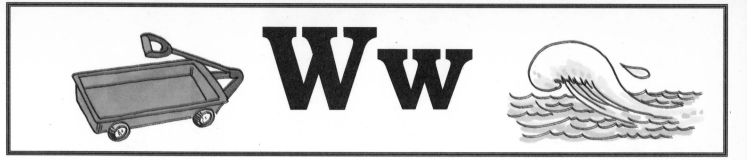

Ww

Wagon

> LET'S PRETEND WE'RE PIONEERS.

Wagons are carts that you use to carry things. **Wagons** don't have engines, so they have to be pulled. Pioneers moved to the western states in **covered wagons**.

Wake
(wakes, woke, woken, waking)

Ricki was sleeping, but **woke up** when the alarm clock rang. Every morning, the alarm clock **wakes** her in time for breakfast.

> WHAT WOULD I DO WITHOUT YOU?

> PROBABLY OVERSLEEP!

> WALKING IS LIKE HAVING YOUR OWN BUILT-IN TRANSPORTATION SYSTEM.

Walk
(walks, walked, walking)

When you **walk**, you use your feet and legs to move from one place to another.

Want
(wants, wanted, wanting)

When you **want** something, you would like to have it or to do it very much. Ashton **wanted** a book of magic tricks because she had always **wanted** to do magic.

> IS THERE A TRICK IN HERE FOR MAKING YOUR LITTLE BROTHER BEHAVE HIMSELF?

> MAGIC TRICKS

> HOW DO YOU FEEL ABOUT THE PROGRAM YOU JUST WATCHED ABOUT WHALES?

> I FEEL SEASICK!

Watch
(watches, watched, watching)

When you **watch** a movie, you look at it for a long time, from beginning to end. The children **watched** a program on whales in science class.

Water

Water is a liquid made from two gases—hydrogen and oxygen. Rain clouds mix these two gases into **water**, which falls to the ground as rain or snow. Water makes up about 65% of a person's body, so people need it to live! So do all other plants and animals.

OUR BODIES ARE ABOUT 65% WATER.

I'LL DRINK TO THAT.

Wave

THIS IS A HAPPENING WAVE.

When water moves, it makes **waves**—moving ridges or humps of water. When you **wave** your hands or your arms, you move them back and forth in an arc.

Wear
(wears, wore, worn, wearing)

During the game, Owen **wore** his lucky hat. He **wore** it on his head. This hat was so old, and Owen had **worn** it so often, that it was almost **worn out**.

COME ON LUCKY HAT... DON'T FAIL ME NOW!

Weather

SOMETIMES THE WEATHER REPORT SAYS IT'S GOING TO RAIN EVEN THOUGH THE SUN IS OUT AND THE SKY IS CLEAR.

The **weather report** tells you if it will be sunny or cloudy, rainy or windy. It tells you what the **weather** will be like.

Weird

Gabby saw a **weird**, or strange, light in the room. It looked so **weird**, or mysterious, that Gabby thought it was a ghost.

THIS IS SO COOL AND VERY WEIRD!

WHO'S WEIRD?

Whale

Whales are the largest animals ever—bigger than dinosaurs. **Whales** are mammals, not fish. They breathe air above the water. They also give birth to their babies and nurse them on milk.

WHALES ARE EVEN BIGGER THAN GODZILLA!

NOW YOU'RE JUST BEING WEIRD!

Wheel

Wheels are circular, or round. **Wheels** have an axle, or stick, through the center, and the **wheels** turn around and around this axle. **Wheelchairs** roll on four **wheels** and are used to carry people.

MY TRICYCLE HAS THREE WHEELS.

YOU MUST BE QUIET IN THIS LIBRARY.

WHAT? SPEAK UP! I DIDN'T HEAR YOU!

Whisper
(whispers, whispered, whispering)

When you **whisper**, you speak so softly that people have trouble hearing you.

Whistle
(whistles, whistled, whistling)

When you **whistle**, you force air through your lips to make a sharp, clear sound. A tea kettle **whistles** or makes a **whistling** noise when the water boils.

YOU CAN ALSO BLOW INTO A WHISTLE.

YOUR WIFE IS MY MOTHER.

Wife

Carrie's mother is married to Mr. Anderson. Her mother is Mr. Anderson's **wife**.

Win
(wins, won, winning)

When your team **wins** at soccer, you play so well that you score more goals than the other team.

YOU WON THE GAME FOR US! NICE GOAL!

THAT'S USING YOUR HEAD.

BESIDES WISHING ON A STAR... I'D BETTER STUDY!

Wish
(wishes, wished, wishing)

Jared **wishes** to do well in school. He really wants and hopes to learn a lot. If he **wishes** upon a star, will his **wish** come true?

Wolf

A **wolf** is a meat-eating, wild animal. **Wolves** look like big dogs with thick fur and long, bushy tails. **Wolves** are part of the dog family and travel in groups called packs.

HAVE YOU SEEN THE BIG BAD WOLF?

WE WERE GOING TO ASK YOU THE SAME THING.

MY 17-YEAR-OLD BROTHER IS DATING A WOMAN.

OH, CUT IT OUT! SHE'S ONLY A YEAR OLDER THAN HE!

Woman

When girls grow up, they are adults and they are called **women**. A **woman** is a girl over the age of 18.

Wood

The **wood** of a tree is the hard part underneath the bark. **Wood** is used to make houses and furniture. You use the word "**woods**" to talk about a small forest of trees.

LET'S GO HIKING IN THE WOODS.

SOMETIMES MY FATHER BRINGS HIS WORK HOME WITH HIM. YUMMY!

Work
(works, worked, working)

Catherine's father **works** in a bakery. He is employed at a bakery. He likes his **work**. He uses his hands, especially when the machines aren't **working**, or running.

Write
(writes, wrote, written, writing)

When you **write**, you put words into an order that says something: The words make sense to someone reading them. Sonia **wrote** a story for the school newspaper.

I WANT TO BE A REPORTER WHEN I GROW UP

Wrong

Dawn cheated on her math test. She copied someone else's answers. That was the **wrong,** or bad, thing to do. It was **wrong**, or unfair. And she copied the **wrong,** or incorrect, answers anyway!

EVERYTHING ABOUT THIS MATH TEST WAS WRONG! THE CHEATING... ME NOT STUDYING ... THE ANSWERS I COPIED!

Xx Yy Zz

TOO BAD DOCTORS DON'T HAVE X-RAY VISION!

X-ray

X-rays are a special kind of light that can make photographs of the bones inside your body. The doctor showed Melanie the **x-ray** of her broken arm.

Xylophone

Xylophones are musical instruments. They have a keyboard, made of wooden or metal bars, that plays the musical scale. A **xylophonist** plays by tapping on the bars with wooden mallets.

I'M GOING TO BE THE FIRST ROCK AND ROLL XYLOPHONE PLAYER.

YAWNING IS CONTAGIOUS.

STOP IT! YOU'RE MAKING ME TIRED.

Yawn
(yawns, yawned, yawning)

You **yawn** when you are sleepy or bored. Your brain needs extra oxygen, so you take in a lot of air by opening your mouth and breathing deeply when you **yawn**.

Year

A **year** is about 365 days, or twelve months, or 52 weeks long. It takes a **year** for the earth to travel around the sun. A new **year** begins on January 1 and ends on December 31.

ONLY 52 MORE WEEKS UNTIL MY NEXT BIRTHDAY.

I'M NOT ANGRY! I'M JUST TRYING TO MAKE A POINT!

THE ONLY POINT YOU'VE GOT IS THE ONE ON TOP OF YOUR HEAD!

Yell
(yells, yelled, yelling)

Sometimes, when people are angry, they **yell** at each other. They argue in a loud voice.

Yo-yo

Sandy got a **yo-yo** for her birthday. She put the string around her finger and moved the **yo-yo** up and down for an hour. It was the only toy of all her gifts. The others were clothes.

A YO-YO IS A VERY RELAXING TOY.

WITH A LITTLE PAINT I CAN TURN YOU INTO A ZEBRA!

Zebra

Zebras are grass-eating animals from Africa. **Zebras** look like white horses with stripes.

Zero

Zero comes before the number one. Nigel had one sticker but gave it to Chester. He then had **zero** stickers. He had none.

YOU JUST GAVE AWAY YOUR LAST STICKER.

HEY! WHAT CAN I SAY? THAT'S JUST THE KIND OF GUY I AM!

MY WINTER JACKET HAS A ZIPPER.

Zipper

Zippers are used like buttons or laces, to hold pieces of clothing together. **Zippers** are made of metal or plastic. They have teeth that lock together as you **zip** the **zipper**.

Zoo

Different kinds of animals are kept at the **zoo**, so people can watch and learn about them. Simon and his grandma fed goats at the children's **zoo**!

THANKS FOR TAKING ME TO THE ZOO, GRANDMA!

I HAD FUN, TOO.

IT'S NOT A GOOD IDEA TO GO ZOOMING THROUGH A NEIGHBORHOOD!

Zoom
(zooms, zoomed, zooming)

The sports car **zoomed**, or went very fast, down the street. Right after that, Ari saw a police car **zoom** by on a wild car chase!